Pets in my house

Goldfish

Jennifer Blizin Gillis

www.raintreepublishers.co.uk

Visit our website to find out more information about **Raintree** books.

To order:

☎ Phone 44 (0) 1865 888112

🗎 Send a fax to 44 (0) 1865 314091

💻 Visit the Raintree Bookshop at **www.raintreepublishers.co.uk** to browse our catalogue and order online.

First published in Great Britain by Raintree, Halley Court, Jordan Hill, Oxford OX2 8EJ, part of Harcourt Education.
Raintree is a registered trademark of Harcourt Education Ltd.

Editorial: Catherine Clarke and Daniel Cuttell
Design: Michelle Lisseter
Picture Research: Jill Birschbach and Maria Joannou
Production: Amanda Meaden

Originated by Dot Gradations Ltd
Printed and bound in China by South China Printing Company

ISBN 1 844 43573 3 (hardback)
09 08 07 06 05
10 9 8 7 6 5 4 3 2 1

ISBN 1 844 43579 2 (paperback)
10 09 08 07 06
10 9 8 7 6 5 4 3 2 1

British Library Cataloguing in Publication Data
Blizin Gillis, Jennifer
Goldfish. – (Pets in my house)
639.3'7484
A full catalogue record for this book is available from the British Library.

Acknowledgements
The publishers would like to thank the following for permission to reproduce photographs: Alamy p.**10** (Jim Nicholson); Alpine Aperture p.**7** (Will and Lisa Funk); Dwight Kuhn p.**6** (right); Getty Images pp.**4** (The Image Bank/Don Klumpp), **20** (National Geographic/ Paul A. Zahl), **22** (PhotoDisc Blue); Harcourt Education Ltd pp.**5** (Dave Bradford), **6** (Greg Williams), **11** (Greg Williams), **13** (Greg Williams), **14** (Greg Williams), **15** (Greg Williams), **16** (Greg Williams), **17** (Greg Williams), **18** (Greg Williams), **19** (Greg Williams), **21** (Greg Williams), **23(a)** (Greg Williams), **23(b)** (Greg Williams), **23(d)** (Greg Williams), **23(e)** (Greg Williams), **23(f)** (Greg Williams), **23(g)** (Greg Williams), back cover (Greg Williams); Hera Bell p.**8**; Photo Edit p.**9** (Michael Newman); Tudor Photgraphy p.**12**.

Cover photograph reproduced with permission of Getty images (Taxi).

The publishers would like to thank Michaela Miller for her assistance in the preparation of this book.

Every effort has been made to contact copyright holders of any material reproduced in this book. Any omissions will be rectified in subsequent printings if notice is given to the publishers.

The paper used to print this book comes from sustainable resources.

Contents

Some words are shown in bold, **like this**.
You can find them in the glossary on page 23.

What kind of pets are these?

Pets are animals that live with people.

Some pets are soft and furry.

My pets are small and slippery.

Can you guess what kind of pets they are?

What are goldfish?

standard

fancy

Goldfish are a type of fish called carp.

There are standard and fancy goldfish.

There are big and little goldfish.

Some big goldfish live outside in garden ponds.

Where do goldfish come from?

Female fish lay eggs on plants in an **aquarium**.

The eggs are picked up with a **net**.

Tiny, pale **fry** come out of the eggs.

When they are about fifteen days old, they can be kept as pets.

How big are my goldfish?

A **fry** is about as long as the end of your finger.

In ten days, it grows to be as big as your whole finger.

My goldfish are grown up.

They are about as long as an adult's finger.

Where do my goldfish live?

aquarium

gravel

My goldfish live in an **aquarium**.

There is **gravel** in the bottom to keep the aquarium clean.

I put plants in the aquarium.

This gives my fish a place to hide.

What do my goldfish eat?

fish food

Goldfish eat special fish food.

They only eat a very small bit at a time.

I sprinkle the food on top of
the water.

The goldfish come straight away!

What else do my goldfish need?

filter

Goldfish need clean water.

This **filter** helps keep the **aquarium** water clean.

air pump

Fish need lots of air to breathe.

This **air pump** puts bubbles of air into the aquarium.

What can I do for my goldfish?

vacuum

I can clean the **aquarium** every day.

This special **vacuum** cleans up dirt and food.

I change some of the water
every week.

I wash the aquarium and put
clean water in.

How are my goldfish special?

Goldfish can be many colours.

They can have spots or shiny patches.

When goldfish sleep, their colour is not as bright.

When they wake up, their colour comes back.

Goldfish map

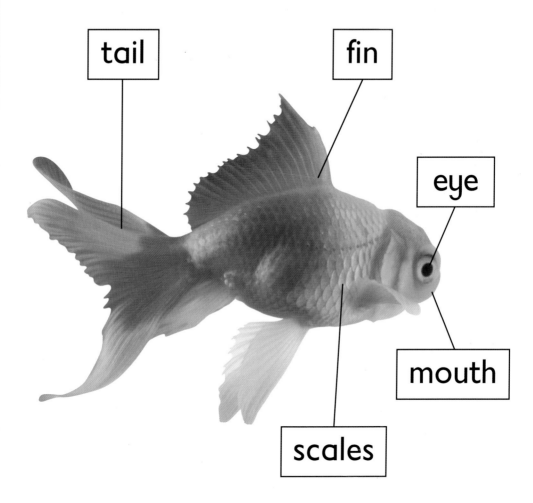

tail

fin

eye

mouth

scales